# How to Act Elegantly Everywhere!

## Manners & Etiquette for Every Occasion

*Elegance Series – Book 2*

By

## Virginia Lia

VIRGINIA LIA

**How to Act Elegantly Everywhere!**

Copyright © 2019

ISBN: 9781700096869

**Warning and Disclaimer**

**Publisher contact**

Skinny Bottle Publishing

books@skinnybottle.com

# Chapter 1

## Manners and Etiquette – What's the difference?

Did you know that you could have good manners, but also be lacking in etiquette? From an early age, we're all taught to have proper manners – thanking someone for holding the door open as we hurry to catch it, sharing toys with your childhood friend, or even saying please when an item is offered.

As you grow older, you notice how good manners are rewarded with equally positive experiences. Socially, if you have good manners you're looked upon with favor, while if you exhibit poor manners you'll likely experience some type of repercussion – whether it's a dirty look, criticism or finding that no one wants to help you when you need it.

But why do we need manners and what good do they do? Imagine for a moment everyone acted as they wished without a care to what society had to say. While we want to say that we would still be well-behaved, chances are most of us would eventually learn to be completely self-absorbed and not give a darn about our neighbor! That's nothing to be ashamed of – it's just human nature.

Now imagine a time in which you've heard something crass or offensive. You probably thought about how inappropriate it was to say such a thing! While there's always an exception to the rule, most people know the difference between right and wrong, or when to say something and not. But in a world with no manners, that no longer matters. Words and actions would be offensive, creating a constant state of chaos.

From the time you are a child, your parents are instilling manner and values into your everyday routine. These manners are used for a lifetime! It starts with remembering to say 'please' and 'thank you' when someone offers you something or sharing your toy with Johnny in the sandbox because he's arrived at the playground all alone and wants to play with your bucket and shovel.

As you grow up, manners become more complex and evolve into something called etiquette. What does it mean to have good etiquette? It simply means taking the manners you've learned and applying them to various scenarios and interactions with others. Here's a simple way to learn the difference between manners and etiquette:

**Manners – The behavior you exhibit toward others.**

**Etiquette – How you behave in certain situations.**

So, as we mentioned before, you can have proper manners but in a certain circumstance, do something that's not perceived as acceptable by society. Throughout this book, we'll go over various situations from learning proper etiquette in the workplace to learning how to be graceful when entertaining at home or at a special event.

For those new to the world of proper etiquette – or living gracefully in a modern world – a foundation of manners and common courtesy is a good place to start.

## What are Manners and Etiquette?

In today's society, what might have been okay to say or do 20 years ago might not be acceptable now. Think about all that's changed in the last 20 to 30 years – with the advancement of technology and social media, it could be hard for the average individual to keep up with manners and etiquette.

Another way to illustrate the concept of manners and etiquette is to think about the last few generations and all that's changed from then until today – in the Victorian ages, etiquette and manners is drastically different than the 21st century! We're much more causal and social now than ever before, but that does not mean that proper manners and living gracefully need to be tossed out the window.

So, it makes sense that the idea of manners changes along with the times in which you live – of course, there are always the basics such as please and thank you, but much of today's manners depend heavily on society as it is now. On the other hand, etiquette is something that doesn't change too much over the years – it includes impeccable manners, being civil to one another, and exuding a sense of courtesy and thoughtfulness to your peers.

In today's more causal world, the idea of etiquette might sound stuffy and snobby, but it's not. It's about making those around you feel welcome and comfortable, whether it's at work, home or even at the coffee shop with a girlfriend. Etiquette isn't something that just rich people have access to – no matter who you are, what your socioeconomic background is, or where you live, you can exhibit grace and elegance through practicing proper etiquette!

Why is it so important to have etiquette and proper manners? In its most simple form, it can be seen as a foundation for other social behaviors and interactions. When there's etiquette involved, it makes communication and interacting with others easier and less awkward – isn't that a good thing? Etiquette also allows us to take other cultures, beliefs, and behaviors into consideration. When you travel, there's a whole world of customs and etiquette that you should know in order to not be offensive or rude – and the same goes for your own native surroundings.

## Manner Essentials

Do you ever think about being rude to someone just because you feel like it? Okay, while it might be super tempting to yell at that man who cut you off in traffic or hurry to close the elevator door before a group of strangers transforms your once quite car into a sardine can, chances are you don't wake up and set out to be rude to everyone who comes into your path. Sometimes we find ourselves in a situation and don't respond the right way for a variety of reasons.

However, there are some of the most basic words and actions that set the foundation for proper manners and are used numerous times throughout a given day, including:

**Excuse me** – This phrase is said for a variety of reasons, whether it's to acknowledge an error was made, you need to get someone's attention, or you must exit and don't want to abruptly leave an interaction or gathering.

**Please** – Do you remember your mother or father telling you that 'please' was a magic word? Or that you would be rewarded when you added please to your sentence, rather than getting what you wanted because you demanded it? At it's most basic level, the use of the word please sets apart your request with a level of respect and mindful consideration.

**Thank you** – How many times a day do you say thank you? Though we know it's expected of us when a person gives us a gift or a favor, there are plenty of other times to bestow some thanks – holding the door open for you, giving you directions when you appear lost, or complimenting your work.

**I'm Sorry** – Sometimes, one of the hardest things to say is 'I'm sorry.' But being able to say it when you understand that you've done something wrong or to hurt (purposely or inadvertently) another person shows maturity and compassion. Additionally, we say 'I'm sorry' in times of grief or sadness – often just these two simple words are all you can say to let someone know that you empathize in their pain.

When it comes to having good manners and etiquette, it's also about feeling as though you can accept credit when it's given to you. Do you feel embarrassed when someone says 'thank you' for a job well done? Do you try to brush it off as if it were nothing?

Accepting compliments is one way to be gracious and live elegantly. When you tell someone, 'Oh, it was nothing' or 'no trouble at all' what you are implying is that being thoughtful or helpful has no value – and it does! Whether you take time out of your day, put someone else's needs or comforts over your own or go above and beyond to make sure something is taken care of, you did go that extra mile and if your peer is giving you thanks, then it's completely alright to accept it with graciousness!

## Understanding Your Boundaries

There's a fine line between doing all you can to make others comfortable and putting yourself last on a constant basis. One of the trickiest aspects of communication is understanding when to say 'no' – how many times have you taken on extra work or stress because you had a hard time turning the request down? More often than not, we all have a hard time saying no without seeming rude, but it's important to know that honesty is a real foundation for proper manners and etiquette.

Suppose there's an office party that needs to be planned at work and you're completely swamped with a final project that needs to be completed in a short amount of time. The original party planner steps down, leaving a void and no one else is stepping up to fill in. You know there's no logical way that you can plan a party and get your work done by the deadline, but when your boss asks if you can add party planning to your list of things to do, you have a very difficult time saying 'no'.

So, what happens when you're stressed out and overwhelmed? Your attention and focus on the work project begins to wane, the party planning starts to go totally wrong and now you're angry, resentful and exhausted. It's a no-win situation for everyone involved.

How do you get the gumption to say no when it doesn't feel like something you can do? Try some of these suggestions next time you feel like you're being backed into a corner:

**Be direct** – Along with the guilt of saying no comes some of the frequent phrases we use when we want to say 'no' but we don't feel like we can just come out and say it. For example, if someone asks you to plan a party, it might be your instinct to get out of it by saying, 'Oh, well I don't know how to plan a party!" This does two things: first, it leaves the possibility open to you planning the party (which you don't want) and second, it opens the door for the other person to say "it won't be that hard, I can get Janet to help you if you need it." Now you're stuck for a second time trying to avoid planning the party – while it might feel uncomfortable at first, saying 'no' without a wiggle room will help you be more effective in your communication.

**Balance it with a positive** – If saying no makes you feel guilty, a good way to help you establish your boundaries is by pairing the no with something more positive. For example, you can say "No, I don't have time to complete that, but I appreciate you considering me for the task."

**Give yourself time to determine if you can take it on** – If you're uncomfortable with always saying yes or no, one tactic to implement into your communication habits is counting up to 10 before you make a decision. Love planning parties and have a project deadline? Maybe you can do both! Counting to ten will give you a moment to calm your mind, consider the pros and cons, and then make a thoughtful decision that you can be comfortable with no matter what it regards.

## Minding your Manners in Public

Having manners ingrained at an early age sets you up for success. Think back to when you were a child and learning how to say please and thank you with your parents or siblings, then you practiced them in public with school children on the playground. As you got older, those same basics were used over and over again in a variety of situations, whether it was in middle school, college or even the workplace.

The concept of greetings is something so natural, it's difficult to know when you're even doing it. Greeting someone also sets a positive tone to the interaction – such as waving to a neighbor as you go on your morning walk or shaking someone's hand at the start of a business meeting. How do you feel when someone doesn't greet you? If you're like most, you might feel slighted or offended because you start to perceive that the individual doesn't like you or is just plain rude.

Greetings – along with other forms of manners – don't always need to be spoken to be understood. Take, for example, the wave of your hand as you pass your neighbor. They might be mowing the lawn and won't hear your shout of greetings over the motor, but with a friendly wave, they understand the implication of your greeting. As with all things manners and etiquette, greetings can be casual or formal, depending on the setting.

By now you may have realized that the basics of proper etiquette is to understand the foundations of manners – these common courtesies are universal. Whether you visit Egypt, China or Brazil, 'please' and 'thank you' are spoken in dozens of languages, but all mean the same thing. Throughout the rest of this book, we'll go over various scenarios and settings in which you'll use many of these basic manners and how to do so with grace and elegance.

# Chapter 2

## What Does it Mean to Act Elegantly?

When you think of the word elegance, what comes to mind? For most, elegance is synonymous with other words, such as sophistication, grace, and style – someone who's elegant acts with class and an air of refinement.

Throughout history, elegance and grace has been observed and marveled over, whether it's in relation to royal families and aristocrats to famous starlets and wives of political figures. What sets someone apart as elegant? In it's most basic definition, elegance is well-defined as having consistency and simplicity. In fact, if you look the word up in the dictionary, it describes elegance as being 'polished with refined grace, as in manners.' Someone who's mature, thoughtful and goes above and beyond with daily routines and manners are more likely to exhibit an elevated sense of taste. Some of the most famous fashion designers agree that elegance isn't something you can wear or the amount of money you have, but rather what type of emotions and behaviors you exude.

Ellie Saab, a designer to some of the best-known actresses and notable figures in modern history, describes elegance like this: *"Elegance is a statement, an attitude. Elegant women are women of character with confidence."*

Elegance is more of a state of mind, rather than an appearance or wardrobe you can purchase from your favorite department store. You can wear the most expensive garments and live in the most beautiful city in the world – but if you don't act with grace and refinement, then elegance will not automatically appear. This means that anyone can act elegantly, no matter where they live and what type of background they have.

Having a good foundation of etiquette and manners sets you up for success when you have the goal to live and act more elegantly. After all, there's nothing you can buy or do that will give you more elegance! While many of the notable figures who exude elegance – women like Grace Kelly or Princess Diana – have been famous and well-off, it's often their demeanor and refinement of personality that gives them that distinction, rather than what material possessions they have at their disposal.

So, what does it mean to act elegantly? Consider these various behavior traits and incorporate them into your daily life:

### Don't Waste Time

Most of us do this on a daily basis – and it's truly a waste of potential. Evaluate your life and figure out where you're spending a good portion of your day that's not bringing you any benefit. One of the most common ways to waste time is to spend it on social media, scrolling and being judgmental of other people's lives, feeling envious over what some people have that you don't, or just wasting time on looking at things you don't truly care about in the long run.

Instead of spending an unlimited amount of time watching television or engaging in social media, use that time to better your skills. Whether you want to learn a new language, read a book or start working on a project you've always wanted to try, there are plenty of things that enhance your overall life and enhance it with elegance.

Not sure whether something is a waste of your time? The best way to determine if it's growing your sense of elegance is to ask yourself this simple question: Is this making me a better version of myself or not? If the answer is no, try to pivot your attention to something that will help you answer yes.

### Mind Your Own Business

Okay, this might sound a bit harsh – but it's true! An elegant individual doesn't worry about what everyone else around them is doing because they are more focused on their own life and trying to make improvements where they can.

Think about the reasons why you might be enticed to watch others – often it's because we are envious of what they are doing or we're trying to make sure we 'stay in the know.' However, acting elegantly means rising above what others are doing and focus on what you are doing to reach goals or to live a more refined life, as mentioned in the previous section.

### Worry less

Sometimes it's easier said than done, but worrying over things you cannot control is a waste of time – and an elegant individual does not waste time! Instead, living gracefully means focusing on what you can control and paying attention to your own life so that you can make changes or adjustments where it is needed.

That's not to say that even an elegant person cannot worry. Sometimes life does cause situations where stress and worries arise, and that's okay. When that happens, it's important to give yourself a little grace and understanding. Instead of dwelling on the area of worry, shift your focus onto the things that are good and going well in life – the things you do have control over.

This also means avoid trying to control other people's actions. While we always want to help those who might need it, the truth is people only change their behavior when they want to – so how does an elegant individual work with this? Instead, he or she will focus on how they accept behavior from others, whether it's by creating boundaries or surrounding themselves with people who inspire them, rather than distract from living their best life.

### Don't live in the past

Living through past mistakes or lost opportunities is hard enough, but dwelling on it throughout life makes it even harder because, at that point, nothing can be done to change it. An elegant person doesn't use the past to define their potential – any mistakes or lost opportunities were lessons learned that carried them to where they are today.

13

Using the past to gain wisdom and grace is ideal, but dwelling only leads to feelings of disappointment. Instead, in order to act more gracefully and elegant, look forward to the future and all of the possibilities that are still out there to obtain, both on a professional and personal level.

### Flaunting is not elegant

As mentioned earlier, living elegantly isn't about what you have, it's about how you behave and exude confidence. For that reason, someone who is elegant never has the need to flaunt material possessions because to him or her, they don't define who they are as people.

This is very evident in the comparison of 'old money' and 'new money' – those with old money, such as royals or others of prominence, don't feel the need to show it off and instead keep their wealth a secret from the rest. Those who have new money are often referred to as 'nouveau riche' which means they like to show others what they have and in some cases, go so far as to flaunt it.

You can be wealthy or poor and still have elegance – it's about not using your material possessions as a way to define just how wonderful you are to others. Designer labels, jewelry, cars...these things don't tell others who you are, they just show them what you have and in the scheme of life, it often means nothing.

### Simplicity is key

When you think of acting with elegance, do you think that means you have to do it all? Quite the contrary. In fact, elegance is about doing more with less – it's about saying no to things that won't be the best use of time or not feeling the need to attend every party just so you don't feel like you're missing out on something.

What happens when you start to do things because you worry about how it will be received? Suppose you attend every party you're invited to, even if you don't want to go or have things to do that will bring you true happiness? You're spending your time feeling bored and resentful – which does not lead to elegant living. It also means you're behaving in a way that no longer helps you grow as a person!

The idea of simplicity also translates to daily life. Why make it harder for yourself when you don't have to? Working is important and key for getting ahead – but working smarter, not harder is essential. Discipline, organization, and lack of clutter in the mind is one of the best ways to be the most productive. Always be willing to get rid of things that don't bring you happiness or growth, whether it's a material object or something more emotional.

## Elegance does not equal perfection

Have you often thought that you can't be elegant because living up to such a level of perfection just seems so unattainable?

It's easy to understand. For a good many people, elegance is about looking perfect every time you step out of the house. How exhausting must it be to think you have to have a full face of makeup or perfectly styled hair just to run a few errands? Those who think they need to be perfect are trying much too hard to live elegantly and they are completely missing the point. Of course, looking clean and presentable is ideal for each person, but no one has to feel the need to be 'perfect.'

Instead, elegance is about being willing to accept oneself – confidence and self-esteem to love everything about who you are, the good and the bad. After all, aren't those traits what make you different from one person to the next? Being comfortable in your own skin is one of the best things you can do to begin living an elegant life.

Gratefulness also sets one apart from others – when you focus on the good things in your life, it leaves you feeling happier and more appreciative of all the other things going on. This demeanor has a major impact on your emotions and overall sense of happiness, which in and of itself, helps you create an aura of elegance!

As you go through this book, keep these tenets of elegance in mind as you navigate through various life changes, major events, and social interactions with others. While etiquette and manners are a great foundation for elegance, you cannot simply just focus on one without the other. Likewise, elegance is not found on its own and takes a level of self-confidence along with proper manners in order to create a well-rounded embodiment of grace and refinement.

# Chapter 3

## Communicating Effectively with Grace and Elegance

There's really no way to integrate into society without communicating. Whether you communicate face-to-face, send notes and stationery, or engage socially through more modern means, such as text message or email, there are numerous ways to do it effectively and properly. One aspect of communication that many people struggle with is personal interaction – small talk or socializing at events.

As a society, we need to communicate. It's the only way to pass information between one another in order to achieve goals and activities, in addition to warning each other about danger or the teaching and passing of knowledge. Connections are also made through communication. Think about the last time you had a conversation with someone and learned that you both loved the same book or television show. It bonded you and created the first signs of a foundation in friendship.

Throughout this chapter, we'll go over all the various ways to communicate with others – how to engage in conversations, what to do when you need to send an email and even how to send a thank you card and notes before or after a special event. As with many aspects of etiquette, there's an informal and formal way to communicate depending on the setting or situation, which we will also go over in this chapter.

## Navigating Small Talk

Being in an unknown social setting is stressful enough, but what happens when you need to engage with others rather than stand alone in that dark corner of the room? While you might naturally be outgoing and can strike up a conversation no matter where you are, most people find it difficult to approach a complete stranger and suddenly find things to say.

Before you step foot in a social event, it's a good idea to understand the foundations of conversation – by understanding certain facets of the situation, you can be armed with knowledge and take some of the stress out of small talk. Instead of putting so much pressure on yourself to figure out what to talk about, it's a good idea to approach small conversation much like you would with someone you do know.

For example, think about when you talk to a partner or friend. One of you says something and the other responds or adds something more to the conversation, allowing you to provide more input or take the conversation in new directions. More often than not, you're engaging in small talk with your friends and family – so what makes it so stressful when you're talking to strangers? Of course, there's a level of comfort and familiarity that you're used to when talking to friends that you don't have when you begin a conversation with someone knew.

So what are some things you can do to make small talk a little less painful? Let's go over some of the basics:

### Body Language

You can tell a lot about the conversation based on body language. Is the person you're speaking to giving you undivided attention? Are they distracted and not making eye contact with you? Are they smiling or not? These are all cues you can use to determine how to navigate small talk.

Introverted individuals or those who aren't as socially outgoing as others find it difficult to maintain eye contact for a long period of time. You don't need to engage in a staring contest with someone to have effective communication, but you should make it a point to have eye contact every so often. One good way of taking the pressure off of communication is to mirror what the other person is doing. Do they make eye contact and then look away for a few moments? You could do the same.

Smiling is another part of body language that plays a major role in small talk. No one really wants to approach someone with a scowl on their face so it's also something to keep in mind when you're in a social setting. Friendly, relaxed body language makes it easier for those to approach you, and vice versa.

Body language also depends on gender. In most cases, women are okay with talking in closer proximity and facing each other, while men tend to stand in a 'V' shape which allows them to make occasional eye contact without giving the appearance of being confrontational.

### Tone

Much like body language, tone is important in conversation – especially small talk. Some say that the tone of your voice adds more to the conversation than the words! While you might be more aware of how your tone comes across in a face-to-face conversation, it's something to be aware of when talking on the phone. Try this exercise: While smiling, say the phrase 'how are you doing today' and then try it again, this time without smiling. Could you detect a drastic difference in the tone of your words? Aside from the physical changes – which are important when communicating in person – your tone can be changed without you even realizing it.

### Word Choice

Grace and elegance is as much about knowing how to act as it is about understanding what to say when you're around others. Consideration is one of the foundations of etiquette, so communicating with others is about using the right words in front of your peers.

For example, how you talk in front of your best friend might be drastically different than the way you speak to your boss. In the case of conversing with your boss, you're able to use industry-specific terms and concepts that, let's say, someone you're sitting next to at a wedding reception won't undersand. Proper etiquette dictates that you try to make those around you comfortable, so you wouldn't use language or terms that they wouldn't understand.

One common culprit of conversation is having too many verbal tics that diminish the quality of the communication. Saying 'umm,' 'like' and other frequently overused terms should be cut out of your vocabulary. First, it's a good idea to know when you say them and make a conscious effort to slow down your speech so that you have time to think about what you want to say rather than fill it with dead words.

## Proper Etiquette on the Internet

The Internet and social media have given all of us much more freedom for communication, but it's still important to employ tactics for elegance and grace. Whether you're sending emails as a professional or in your personal life, there are plenty of tips for making sure your emails are effective and match the tone that you need.

### *Email*

Depending on whom you're sending an email to, your tone and language may vary. Emails aren't meant to be lengthy documents full of text, but rather short and concise messages that can be read and responded to quickly. The recipient of your email will also determine how you address the body of the text. In more formal emails, you'll typically start the email out with the traditional salutation, 'Dear' followed by the title of the person you are addressing.

If you're emailing a colleague or friend, you can start the email with the recipients first name – but make sure they know who you are. Don't assume that everyone will be on a first-name basis with you, especially if the email is the first point of contact.

Once your email is complete, you'll want to finish it with a closing message. This option depends again on who you're emailing – for example, if it's a professional cover letter or another type of business email, closing the body of text with 'Sincerely or 'Regards' is fairly standard practice. Emailing a causal friend or colleague? Close out the email with something a little less formal, such as 'Best.'

A variety of email features are available to help you in different situations and proper etiquette is required when deciding to use some of them! One of the most popular features is 'CC,' which is also known as carbon copy. This is used when you want to share your email with more people than just the original recipient – typically if you're in a group email about a work or school project or perhaps you're in a family email about a certain situation that needs more than one input.

When utilizing the CC feature, proper etiquette means that you only include those on the email list who have given you permission to do so. The CC feature shows everyone in the message all of the emails included – not everyone is keen with their email address floating around, especially to people they might not know. Another feature, known as 'BCC,' or blind carbon copy, allows you to send the email to everyone on the list without the email addresses being visible to one another. This is a good way to send out emails while also keeping addresses private.

One downside to using CC or BCC features is that they can be tricky to navigate and when a response is sent to the original message, all the email recipients get the message. Be cautious about how you reply to such emails and only hit the 'Reply All' tab when everyone on the list needs to see your response. Otherwise, respond directly to the message you need to correspond with and avoid annoying all of your peers – the last thing anyone wants is a deluge of emails with scattered responses.

While there are proper etiquette standards for sending email, there are also a few tips and guidelines for dealing with messages once they hit your inbox. Due to the nature of email, responses are usually needed and, preferably, done within a respectable amount of time. Of course, a good portion of your messages can be responded to quickly – but what happens when your message is requesting information, or you need some extra time drafting a response? Do you just let that email sit there until you're ready to deal with it? No.

One way to be courteous to the sender is to let them know that the message has been received, but that you will need some time creating the response – this helps them know you got the email (so they don't feel like they need to send a duplicate message) and it also gives you the opportunity to draft a quality response and it shows you're being respectful of their time.

### Text Message

Even though email is designed to be quick and to the point, text messages are even shorter and are much more informal as a whole. They're designed to elicit a quick response – such as where you're parked, how long you'll be, or even conversing with a friend in short snippets of text.

One major downside to the idea of text messages is that they are often the source of misunderstanding. With rapid lines of text going back and forth, there are a lot of things missing that you'd find in face-to-face communication: especially body language and tone. There are also boundaries to sending informal communication, such as text messages.

Proper etiquette for sending messages is to know who the recipient is. Are they frequently on their phone or do they generally avoid doing anything except making phone calls? Their phone habits can let you know whether they'll even see a text message or if you're better off calling. If your text message requires a lengthy response or if you find that your message is too long, the texting format might not be the best avenue.

Finally, there's a time and a place where texting – or being on the cellphone in general – is acceptable and not. A movie theater or other dark environment is no place for the glowing lights of your cellphone screen! Texting and driving is also off-limits, as it creates a distraction that could leave you in a disastrous situation.

No matter how you communicate, it's important to consider your surroundings and needs. Etiquette also has a lot to do with personal choices – how do you want your communication to reflect on you? Whether you're text messaging or engaging in small talk, the way you speak or send messages highlights your personality and communication.

# Chapter 4

## Acting Gracefully in the Workplace

Within the last few decades, the entire concept of professional life has completely changed. At one time, you would graduate college, enter a professional career and stay there until you retired; however, staying at one job for the entirety of your life is not only unrealistic, it's fairly unattainable now. That means that over the course of your life, you'll apply to numerous jobs, go through frequent interviews and even attend a fair share of professional events and company parties.

Etiquette in the workplace is just as important as infusing grace and elegance into other areas of your life. Professionally, a good reputation is much more beneficial and respected than not – and with the constantly changing landscape of business life, you don't have the time and luxury to re-invent yourself and your reputation once it's established.

Whether it's fair or not, co-workers, employers, and other business professionals are constantly watching and

25

judging others based on manners and etiquette and while that might add an element of stress to your work life, there's some good news: these judgments are often based on what employers and co-workers see, which means you control your own reputation.

Is etiquette really that important in the workplace, you might wonder? For a moment, think about the business professionals and employers that you've seen and respected. What have they done to gain such a favorable view in your eyes? Is it because they acted respectfully and with consideration? Or perhaps they appear at working looking sharp and put together?

Throughout this chapter, we'll go over some of the fundamentals for etiquette when it comes to navigating various work events and situations.

## Beginning the Job Process

First impressions are everything – and they can often mean the difference between getting the job and not when there are others as equally qualified as you for a position. With the high amount of competition for a limited number of jobs, etiquette and professional manners tend to go further in the long run.

Searching for a job isn't just about printing out a resume and hoping you'll get an interview. It's also an opportunity to network and use the contacts you have to create leads. For the case of this chapter, we'll assume that there are no possible leads or contacts for you to utilize – so what do you do?

If you're interested in working with a specific company, connecting with the business directly as opposed to looking at open job listings on a website does have the potential for advantage – but only if done so with the proper manners and etiquette. Before you decide to send a cold phone call, letter or email (which means you're sending communication without a prior connection with the potential individual), you need to call the business and determine who the hiring or department manager is and the correct spelling (or pronunciation) of their name. You certainly don't want to be connected to the hiring manager in charge and mispronounce their name – it will definitely leave a bad impression and highlight the fact that you don't pay much attention to the details.

There's also a fine line between being persistent and obnoxious when trying to obtain information about a potential opening or trying to communicate with the hiring manager. One good rule of thumb is to only make phone calls three times per month – if you still have trouble connecting with the person you need to speak with, consider asking the assistant or secretary when a good time to call is. This could help you be a bit more successful when calling and prevent you from appearing too desperate.

When you finally have a chance to connect with the person in charge, be mindful of their time. Proper etiquette means that you speak in a relaxed, friendly tone and provide concise information – provide your name, your experience, and expertise that's relevant to the business and that you're interested in openings or potential openings that arise in the department of choice.

At this point in the phone conversation, the hiring manager could either say they are interested and would like to see your resume or they might tell you there's nothing open and that you might have luck at a later time.

No matter how the phone conversation goes, a written or emailed thank you note is a great way to make a good impression and it helps build a relationship with the individual – both important aspects in the world of business. Writing and sending thank you notes throughout the job-hunting process is one of the key aspects of business etiquette and proper manners. When is it appropriate to send one? Anytime someone helps you – whether it's providing a referral, setting up an appointment or meeting, offering an endorsement or landing a job!

## The Job Interview

Job interviews are often stressful enough without worrying about whether or not you're following proper protocol or etiquette, but many aspects to consider are basics and utilized through many other aspects of communication.

Some of the key things to remember are:

**Dress appropriately for the interview.** While your resume and experience are important, how you present yourself to the interviewers are just as important. Before leaving for the interview, take a look in the mirror as if you were the employer getting ready to hire an individual – would you fit the bill? Your attire offers a first impression before you even have a chance to share your skills and experience. Clothing should also match the environment for which you are interviewing. For example, if you are interviewing for a corporate position, a suit or dress with proper shoes is appropriate. When interviewing at a more casual location, slacks and a collared shirt for men, or a blouse and slacks for women is a suitable option. Proper etiquette means giving off the right impression, so go for more muted styles during the interview process – you don't want your attire taking away from your personality or words!

**Show up on time.** It seems to go without saying that showing up on time is often the difference between getting the job and not. Plan to arrive at the interview location with at least 15 minutes to spare – add even more time if you live in an area with high traffic or you rely on a public transportation system. Always be prepared for the unexpected! If you show up too early to the interview location, scope out an area where you can relax and get into the mental zone and then "arrive" to the interview five minutes early.

Once you're ready to sit down and go through the interview process, your words and actions will be front and center. You'll want to exhibit some level of self-confidence in order to give off the impression that you're well-qualified and capable, but it's important not to appear too arrogant. Preparation before an interview is key to responding to questions with thoughtful answers – while you might not know all of the interview questions, you can prepare answers to some of the most commonly asked, such as what are your greatest strengths and weaknesses, why do you want to be a part of the company, what can you offer in ____ role – knowing how to respond to these type of questions will also help you appear more natural and relaxed during the entire interview.

Another way to prepare for an interview is by reading and understand the purpose of the company. This allows you to ask questions if you have them, but it also shows the interviewers that you have invested time and energy into learning more about them and that always shows great business etiquette.

Other business etiquette basics to keep in mind are highlighting your personal communication skills. For example, a warm smile and a handshake is an ideal way to begin the interview. Look at the interviewer in the eye and address him or her with a greeting, followed by a thank you for setting up the interview. Though you want to remain professional and cordial, you also want to be relaxed and friendly. You might be nervous during the interview process, but it's important not to show it. Smiling frequently throughout the interview highlights your positive energy, which does wonders at creating a positive experience with the others in the room.

Imagine you were sitting in a room and in charge of interviewing someone, but they never smiled – instead, they looked nervous, strained or even shifty with a lack of eye contact. Even if they had the best answers in the world, chances are you'd wonder how they would fit in the company and whether interpersonal communication is something that could be an issue! No matter how nervous or stressed you might be, smiling will help convey that you're self-confident and enjoying your time (which is the important part in the eyes of the interviewer).

Answering questions is done with a level of finesse. There's a line between self-confidence and bragging – and no one likes a know-it-all. Instead, be sure to answer questions without a condescending tone and if the interviewer offers compliments over your resume or experience, accept it graciously and a simple thank you will suffice, rather than bragging about your accomplishments.

After the interview process, a thank you note is recommended for a variety of reasons. First, it will once again show the interviewer that you're serious about the job and that you're interested, and second, it's proper etiquette when someone takes time to consider you for a position. You'll want to really take advantage of these benefits by sending the thank you note out within a day or two of the interview – any time after that will appear more as an afterthought and not as etiquette in the way it's designed.

But how do you send a thank you note? Does it need to be written or can it be emailed? The answer depends on the company you interviewed with and the way they communicate with you – are they more high-tech and prefer to do all correspondence by email? Then a thank you by email is a good way to go. If you're interviewing for a more conservative business, handwritten notes might be better received – in that case, be sure to email the interviewer later in the day and highlight that a note will be on its way.

In the thank you note, be sure to mention again when you met with the individual, followed by the reason why you met them – if you mentioned anything in the interview, such as showing more pieces to a portfolio or contacting a different member of the team, let them know in the thank you note that you followed up and provide the necessary details.

## Elegance on the Job

After you've been hired, maintaining a professional appearance and ensuring proper communication is essential for success. Common manners in the workplace include doing what you say you'll do, work to solve problems rather than create more of them and treating others around you with respect. On your first day of work in the new office, there are a multitude of emotions to experience – excitement, mixed with a little nervousness, after all – you're meeting people who you'll spend a good portion of your days and weeks with over the course of the year.

A first impression is important in the interview room, but it's even more important when you meet your co-workers for the first time. While there's always the chance where some co-workers might not be as receptive to you at first, here are some basic manners to follow in order to set a great first impression.

**Be on time.** Whether it's your first day of work or you've been working there for years, always be on time for every appointment or meeting. Your time is valuable and so is the time that belongs to the people waiting for you – one of the core attributes of manners and etiquette is being respectful of others and when you're late, you're inadvertently telling them that their time isn't that important to you.

**Always dress the part**. If you have a work uniform or you're allowed to dress how you want, always err on the side of professionalism. When you're not sure if a certain garment is work-appropriate, take a look in the mirror and observe yourself as others would see you. Does that blouse look professorial or are your khaki pants a little worse for wear? If you see an issue with your wardrobe, chances are your bosses and co-workers will see it, too. Also, it's not always about whether you like something or not – it's about whether your garments fit the environment of the office or place of business.

**Remember names.** If you have some time between hiring and the first day of work, use that as an opportunity to get to know others in your department and to make sure you know how to pronounce your boss' name. Learning these things ahead of time takes a little pressure off your first day of work.

In some cases, the position for which you've been accepted is as a manager or supervisor. In addition to first-day jitters, you could also experience a sense of nervousness over being a new boss to those you've never met and you want to set a good impression with the team. Even though you're in an elevated position within the company, you do owe it to the team to be respectful and show proper etiquette if you want to set a good impression.

Here are some etiquette tips for being an effective boss:

**Be available to your team members.** There's nothing worse than a boss who's never around – it lowers moral amongst the team and your employees start to lose respect for you. There's a balance between being available and being a micromanager, so let them know you can be reached when they have an issue and be sure to schedule in face time, if necessary.

**Offer compliments.** One way to connect with your team is to understand their skills and give compliments when they are deserved. This shows them that you know when they go above and beyond – which is a great way to build high morale.

**Don't pass mistakes off to others.** If a mistake occurs on your team, own up to it and don't pass it off to someone else. Doing this will cause your team to think you lack integrity and it shows that you can't take criticism yourself when something goes wrong. If you're the manager or boss, you should accept mistakes and implement a procedure to keep it from happening again.

**Keep your communication clear.** When you talk with an employee, they need to hear duties and instructions in clear, concise language to avoid mistakes or misunderstandings. Never sugarcoat or beat around the bush when you need to correct mistakes or deliver bad news – this only muddies the message further and leads to confusion.

**Always treat others with respect.** No matter where an employee is on the hierarchy of the company, proper business etiquette means that you treat everyone with the same manners and respect. Say please and thank you to all workers and provide them with your attention when they come to you to speak about an issue. Respect is one of the key qualities for a manager, so you need to work hard at keeping it.

Etiquette in the workplace also means keeping your desk or common spaces clean and organized. Clean up after yourself in the breakroom, empty out the refrigerator of your days-old food, and wipe up any messes if you make them. No one at the office is there to clean up your mess, so you must be respectful and not treat the common areas as your own personal space.

Organization is another major component of office etiquette – stay on top of meetings in order to avoid being late or taking up too much time from others going over things you should already know. When speaking with others in the office, take special care to listen and not interrupt when they are talking. If you're heading out of the office for a networking event or meeting, always have some business cards on hand to pass around – you could meet new clients or potential suppliers and should always be prepared.

Elegance at the office is just like being mindful and courteous anywhere else. Treat others with respect and dignity so that you are treated in the same fashion. Keep your personal issues away from the office – they might be difficult to deal with, but your office mates don't need to know your personal drama and in many cases, it often causes an awkward work environment. If you develop a friendship with some of your peers, keep personal talk and conversation limited to breaks and lunchtime.

As with any type of communication and interpersonal relationships, learning how to behave properly at the office is done through showing basic manners and etiquette – treat others as you want to be treated! A positive attitude and taking others into account are two ideal ways to create a sense of respect in the workplace – and while it might be a learning curve at first, implementing proper etiquette from the start will set a wonderful foundation moving forward with your co-workers, staff, and bosses.

# Chapter 5

# All Things Wedding

An engagement is one of the most exciting times of your life, followed by a wedding and then all of the major milestones you strive for in a lifetime. While there's no designated length of time for an engagement to last – it could be a few days or last years – the typical engagement time lasts about 14 months. During this time, you have an opportunity to save for the wedding and plan it out or you can choose a future date to accommodate the season and time of year you want to hold the event, or perhaps you have a dream wedding destination and it's booked well in advance.

## Congratulations, You're Engaged!

Engagements can also be shorter due to a number of obligations. If the budget is tight and you don't plan to throw a large wedding, a simple ceremony with friends and family is all you need – so a short engagement makes perfect sense. There could also be external reasons for having a short engagement, such as an intensive school schedule, military service or deployment or even work commitments that you aren't able to postpone.

So where does proper etiquette play a role in the engagement? First and foremost, it's about enjoying this new change in your life with that special someone – and you also need to remember to be considerate and compromise with your partner when necessary. After all, it's not just your wedding!

After the engagement takes place, it's time to share the good news with the rest of the world. But first, it's always proper to tell those who are closest to you – friends and family. Suppose you shared the engagement news on your social media and Grandma Sally found out about your upcoming wedding through Facebook along with all of the other people in your life – old friends from high school, that co-worker you didn't want to accept as a friend, but thought it would be awkward at the office if you didn't...you get the idea. Your family should be the first to know, followed by your closest friends and then the rest of your social circle.

If you have children from a previous relationship or your partner has children, it's of the utmost etiquette to tell them first. This could be a touchy subject for children, especially teenagers who will now have a stepparent or even new stepsiblings, so be sure to create a comfortable environment in which to share the news. Be prepared for them to be happy, but they can also be very upset – it all depends on the family dynamic and how the children have grown up. It's important to be extra considerate in this transition, especially to children because even if it's a positive change, it's a change nonetheless. After telling the children, it's also a good idea to share the news with your former spouse if this is a second marriage as a form of courtesy to the other parent of your child(ren) and keeps them from having to inform their mother or father about the new changes coming.

Once you've shared the engagement news with any children in the relationship, the next group of people to share with are your parents. You can tell your parents on your own or have your partner with you, depending on the established relationships. If your parents haven't met your fiancé, meeting face-to-face with a proper introduction is the most respectful way to go. What happens if your parents live further away or across the country? You can share the news over the telephone, but you should plan to visit at your next available opportunity to allow everyone to meet.

Even though the concept of one suitor talking to the parents before an engagement to ask for a hand in marriage or to share plans isn't done much anymore, it's still a good sign of respect – old fashioned or not. If this conversation doesn't happen before the engagement, it's respectful and considerate to do it even after the engagement news is shared. When and how this conversation takes place depends on the family relationship and how proper you and your future spouse want to be.

Finally, after you've shared your news with family, it's up to you how you want to announce the news to friends and your extended social circle. Keep in mind that during the sharing of your engagement, don't begin to tell others (or promise) to invite them to the wedding – first, you'll end up with an enormous party which could end up quite expensive, and second, you don't want people at your wedding that you had to invite because you promised them in the moment.

This also goes for asking people to be in the bridal party or giving them a verbal invitation. Spend some time thinking about your bridesmaids and groomsmen before even bringing the topic up – the last thing you want to do is have to rescind the honor because you decided that your wedding needed to stay on budget or you didn't have a need for an extended bridal party. The same is true for verbally inviting guests to the wedding – as you plan the event, you might find that catering is much more expensive than you thought, or your dream wedding venue only holds so many people. When sharing the engagement news, keep it only at that: sharing the news.

Even though engagements should be happy and full of love, not all of them have fairy tale endings. There might be a chance where your parents or even children aren't happy or even disapprove of the engagement. Of course, it's very natural to feel betrayed or upset at this news – parents are often not as thrilled as one would hope for very common reasons: they want to make sure you are making the right decisions with your future and committing to the person who suits you best.

If that's the case, many of those anxious thoughts from your parents tend to go away as they get to know your fiancé better (if they don't know them already) and the wedding plans begin. Let's suppose they do know your fiancé and the tension between you grows even deeper during wedding planning – what does proper etiquette indicate you should do?

**Try to remain calm when communicating.** Sure, it's very difficult to plan a wedding to someone you love when your family is creating tension. First and foremost, try to have discussions about the situation in as calm of a manner as possible.

**Consider the concerns.** When you're engaged and excited to be married, the last thing you want to do is hear the reasons why that person isn't a good fit for you. However, always try to listen to the concerns of your parents – through communication, you can address some of those concerns and hopefully put them at ease. For all you know, their concerns might be unfounded because they aren't aware of the full picture of your relationship. At the end of the day, you're an adult and can make whatever decisions you want, but being in love also means sometimes being blinded to red flags that others see. If you hear the concerns and don't find them to affect your decisions, then you've done your part in communicating with your parents.

Navigating family tension is never easy, but it's important not to sever ties completely. If you choose to go on with a marriage, it's considerate to still tell your parents when the wedding date is and leave an open invitation. If children are involved and they are not happy about the upcoming marriage, family counseling could prove to be helpful to improve communication and expectations.

Not all engagements end in a marriage, either. This period of time gives a couple the opportunity to work together planning the wedding and moving on with other life goals together – and sometimes a couple realizes that the relationship just isn't strong enough to continue. A broken engagement could be embarrassing and sad, but it's important not to go through with a wedding just for the sake of avoiding such feelings.

As with all events, there are a few etiquette rules for what you should and shouldn't do after a broken engagement:

**Make the announcement as soon as you are able. Just** as you told your children and parents about the engagement first, they should also be first to learn of the broken engagement. This could be an equally difficult situation for children, especially if they are fond of your partner – talk to them honestly and with respect to the other person, just as you would in the case of a divorce.

**Don't make people pick sides.** Though your friends and family will likely be sympathetic to your broken engagement, don't make them pick a side – especially if they liked your fiancé. Asking your circle of friends and family to pick a side is like asking them to partake in drama that they have no business being a part of.

**Contact wedding vendors.** As soon as you can, contact all of the services and vendors you hired and determine how to go about getting a refund if it's possible. You should also speak personally with each individual who was going to play a part in your wedding day, from the officiant to the bridal party.

**Return any gifts.** The proper thing to do is return any gifts you or your fiancé have received back to the sender. A brief handwritten note should ideally be included and could be worded something like this:

*Dear Sarah,*

*I am sorry to share that John and I have broken our engagement. I am returning the beautiful plates you were so kind to send us.*

*Love,*

*Lindsay*

**Inform the guests.** If invitations have been mailed, then a printed note sent to everyone announcing the broken engagement is courteous. If the wedding guest list was small, a personal phone call is an equally proper notification.

Finally, one of the most notable questions after a broken engagement is: what do I do with the ring? While there is no legal obligation to give the ring back (check with your state legal rules!), the ring was given to you as a symbol of a commitment. When that commitment is broken, there really is no proper need to keep it and it should be given back to your partner. If the ring that was given to you is an heirloom, there is no doubt that it should be given back!

If you and your fiancé purchased the ring together, then it (along with any other jewelry that was given to in a similar fashion) should be sold and the value split between the both of you.

## Wedding Etiquette and Traditions

As we mentioned earlier, etiquette often depends on cultures and customs based on the foundation of manners and proper consideration, and weddings are no different. When it comes to weddings, you can create the event of your dreams, personalizing it with special touches while also including many of the traditions and etiquette that's known to your family or heritage.

New trends also crop up and change the landscape of traditional etiquette and weddings are one area in which modern changes have done away with old fashioned expectations. One way in which this is evident is by sharing the costs of a wedding. In today's economy, weddings can be quite expensive and at one time, a bride's family typically covered the cost – but now modern etiquette has changed the way in which a wedding is paid for or planned.

Traditionally a bride's parents once paid for a good portion of the wedding. With the changes in the economy and couples getting married later in life, there's not always the opportunity to have the wedding costs covered by family. This means the couple often pays for the wedding themselves or takes on the help of both the bride and groom's family.

Another change in wedding etiquette is the fact that more often than not, the wedding is known as an encore event, which means that it's the second or more marriage for the couple – this includes more family, children and a whole host of manners and etiquette that need to be accounted for when planning. Other aspects of modern weddings include choosing green weddings (opting for environmentally-conscious vendors or products), mothers escorting brides down the aisle or the bride selecting both parents, grooms being much more involved in the planning process, and implementing technology in the wedding, such as through announcements or creating a wedding website. Plan on including some unique customs or rituals into your wedding ceremony? A great way to keep your guests in mind is to enlighten them on what to expect, rather than being confused or shocked when an unfamiliar activity takes place – this also helps them feel included in the activity, whether it's watching the lighting of the unity candle or going through some non-religious readings.

## *The Guest List*

There are two elements to be planned for the wedding: the ceremony itself and the reception that follows. Even weddings that are intimate in size take an element of planning – and three facets of etiquette: compromise, consideration, and communication.

Planning a wedding takes a few foundational considerations – the guest list being one of them. The number of people you want to invite to the wedding can have a major impact on your budget, venue location, food selection – even your wedding theme and style! For most couples, the most important part of the day is spending it with friends and family, which is why the guest list often takes precedence in the early stages of wedding preparation.

If you have a large network of friends and family and a modest or small budget, it might be difficult to navigate the guest list. Traditional wedding etiquette recommends breaking the guest list up into different categories, including family, friends, business associates, followed by level of closeness – feelings will be less hurt if a certain category is left off, rather than inviting say one or two of the cousins, but not the other eight you have in the family. Immediate family should always have the first invitations – parents, siblings, grandparents and then any children that either of you brings to the marriage. Next is extended family, followed by friends of the couple and some of the parent's friends. When creating the guest list, you'll also need to accommodate a 'plus-one' for your guests if they have partners or spouses.

## Budgeting Tips

Planning the wedding starts with compromise and consideration, especially when it comes to something as important as the budget. You should always be realistic and considerate when planning – the first step is to create a budget and then divide it by the things you and your partner deem most important. Would you rather have a lavish reception and fewer guests or a more causal wedding that can accommodate all of your friends and family? This is a conversation you need to have with your partner and compromise so you both move forward on the same page.

## Choosing Your Bridal Party

If you have a close-knit family or group of friends, selecting the bridal party could feel like a no-brainer. Where you might run into some trouble is if you have an extensive network of family and friends – this makes selecting a modest bridal party even more difficult.

There's no rule to how many attendants you can have in the bridal party and you don't even need to have an equal number of people on any one side – it's about having the people you love helping you throughout the planning and standing up there with you on the big day! More modern weddings are also doing away with the notion of having only one maid of honor and a best man. Personalize your wedding in a way that makes sense to you as a couple.

Be sure to request your bridal party as soon as possible. This courtesy gives them the opportunity to purchase necessary garments, make travel arrangements and even request time off from work to participate in a number of activities. It's also important to note that not all of your invitations will be accepted – some might not have the ability to take time away from work or families or even have the financial stability to purchase gowns. Even though you will feel disappointed, don't make them feel bad for declining an invitation – it's better to maintain the relationship rather than guilt someone into joining the bridal party and feeling resentful on one of the biggest days of your life.

When you provide the invitation, be sure to let them know all of the details as soon as possible and what you need from them during the wedding – attendants are there to help things run smoothly on the wedding day, so you'll want to tell them of their obligations before they commit. They should also be told of a general budget for their attire, transportation, and other events so they can budget or decline the invitation if spending that money is not possible.

### What do I do after the wedding?

After the wedding day, it's proper etiquette to thank guests for gifts. Thank you notes should be written soon after the wedding – if there are a good number of notes to send out, break it up into small daily amounts until your list is complete. There are a few dos and don'ts when it comes to sending out such notes:

**Always sign the card as both of you** – even if you're writing all of the thank you notes. Writing thank you notes isn't a job for one person, so spend time as a couple writing them – they'll get done much faster!

**Give it some thought** – purchasing a box of thank you cards from the store and simply singing them shows very little in the way of manners. Each note should include thanks for the particular gift, followed by a personal feeling and thankfulness for attending the wedding.

A wedding is one of the biggest days in your life that rests much of its foundation on etiquette and manners – more so than any other event! While you can certainly follow many of the modern traditions and customs, there are still basics in etiquette that should be observed in order to live a more graceful life and carry some of the most notable traditions of consideration.

# Chapter 6

## Family and Living with Others

On a daily basis, you're surrounded by people who know you best – but does that mean there's no element of manners or etiquette to be used? Every home is different, where the customs, traditions, and cultures also vary. When you visit someone's home, you get a good idea about what that person is like – from the physical environment to how you are greeted when you arrive.

If you're a guest in someone's home, it's always expected that you follow whatever traditions or customs that are established in that home. For example, if you arrive at your co-worker's house and his family removes shoes when coming inside, then you will need to do the same in order to be mindful of his space and show proper grace and respect.

Respect and consideration also goes for adults living together in a home. While you both share a single space, creating an environment of thoughtfulness and courtesy goes a long way toward establishing a healthy and calm life at home. How do you act gracefully even if no one's watching?

**Give each other alone time.** Whether you each have separate hobbies or you just need some quiet time after a long day of work, it's considerate to give each other time to spend alone. Though you might think that 'alone time' means your partner wants to get away from you, it's actually good for the relationship to develop interests that don't include the other. This allows each of you to build trust and to remain individuals – which strengthens the overall bond of a relationship.

**Always respect privacy.** Privacy is a big deal for relationships – it might be difficult to consider that your partner doesn't tell you everything. In order to provide the utmost respect, don't go through personal journals or diaries, mail or text messages.

**Respect each other at home and in public.** The way you present yourself and partner shows others how they may receive you. It's not proper to air your dirty laundry in front of others – especially if they are intimate in nature. When in public, also refrain from insulting or putting one another down – aside from it being deeply humiliating, it gives others a bad impression of your relationship.

Maintaining proper manners and etiquette in the home is even more important if there are children present. It's in the home where children learn the foundation of respect and manners – they often imitate what they see and hear, so it's vital that you and the other adults in the home set a good example.

## Dealing with the In-Laws

Does the word 'in-laws' conjure up frightening memories or do you get along well with your partner's parents? After marriage, you gain a set of parents – though they aren't exactly strangers, they do have their own set of customs and traditions that you need to be aware of when interacting with them. As more cultures are blended together through marriage in the coming years, it will be more common than not to be blending a household with religious and cultural traditions.

As is the case with dealing with any person, there are a few basic points of etiquette to implement into your interactions:

**Be tolerant and willing to accept differences. One** of the best ways to keep the peace between families is to avoid interfering or inserting your opinion on everything. Different families have various ways of doing things, so to keep the family peace and your life stress-free, accept the differences and be tolerant even if you don't understand them.

**Don't look for hidden meanings.** It could be difficult to hear what you deem a flippant remark from your mother-in-law, but there's also a good possibility she meant nothing by it. If you look for double meanings in everything your in-laws say, it could lead to an abundance of resentment and create fractures in the relationship – especially if you go to your spouse and want them to pick a side. The best way to manage is to take what they say at face value and let it go – if there truly is a misunderstanding, confront it quickly and with grace so that it doesn't continue over time.

**Don't hold on to grudges.** It's not good for you and it's not good for your relationship – especially because it's your partner's parents and putting him or her in the middle is never a good idea. You have two options – you can talk to your in-laws if it's worth fixing or you can try to move on and give yourself peace of mind.

## Navigating the Milestones

When you belong to a family, whether it's just two of you or a whole host of extended family, there's a vast number of milestones you'll need to remember. From birthdays and anniversaries to graduations and retirements, you'll be busy a good portion of the year marking these special events. Celebrating various milestones with loved ones is something to enjoy – but the whole notion around gift-giving is where it can add a tiny bit of complication.

What happens if you just don't have a spare dollar to get a gift for an upcoming milestone? When you have a large family – not to mention extended family – getting gifts for every birthday and special event could add up to a substantial amount of money each year. Even if you don't have any financial woes, giving flashy and expensive presents isn't exactly recommended, either. It can cause resentment for those who don't have the same opportunity to lavish gifts on a loved one and some family members might see it as you 'showing off.'

One of the best ways to navigate milestones is to follow the lead of other family members. While you definitely want to put a personalized touch on gifts and thoughtful gestures, proper etiquette means that you keep the recipient in mind and consider the other family members when picking out a gift.

## Pregnancy, Adoption, and Birth Announcements

That time of your life has come – you want to bring children into the family! Along with the decision to expand the family, there are a number of questions that you might have, especially as it relates to sharing the news with extended family and friends.

Aside from announcing a pregnancy, birth or adoption, there are other aspects of the special event that also require planning and proper etiquette in order to avoid hurting anyone's feelings. Even though it's completely your choice in how you share the news, it shows good etiquette and grace to tell immediate family first – just as with any other major milestone, you don't want your immediate family members to find out the big news at the same time (or after!) your friends hear about it on social media.

The choice as to when you want to announce your pregnancy, birth or adoption is also up to you – just make sure that your immediate family is first to learn of the news. Every couple has a preference, so there is no ideal timeframe in which to announce your news if you don't feel comfortable sharing. For example, some couples might like to announce the fact they will be trying for a child or submitting the documents in order to be considered for adoption. Others might wait until the first trimester of the pregnancy is complete before feeling comfortable enough to share, while some might even wait until birth or the adoption is finalized before making the announcement. It's all based on personal preference.

In terms of etiquette – it's more about the reception from friends and family that's the important part. While you might be thoroughly excited about the arrival of a new child in the family, it's not appropriate to constantly ask about an update every time you see the individual. Why? For a good number of couples, the process is very private and, for some, can be a very emotional time if they've had difficulty conceiving (which is extremely personal and you can't possibly know what others go through in their private life). Constantly asking for updates or checking in with parents-to-be, whether they are pregnant or going through adoption, is very insensitive and can feel intrusive to the couple.

When it comes to pregnancy, those around you are going to eventually notice that you're getting ready to have a baby – but there are plenty of tips and guidelines to help you and your friends respect boundaries and provide plenty of positivity.

If you're pregnant, here are some tips to helping you navigate through the following months of pregnancy:

> Pregnancy is exciting for you, but don't expect to be the center of attention at all times. This goes for many special events in your lifetime – your friends and family can be happy and excited for your news, but always remember that they have their own life and it's not personal if they don't shower you the attention you perceive you'll get during pregnancy.

Keep some things personal. You'll have ultrasound pictures, pregnancy pictures and even pictures of your newborn, but don't feel obligated to share them with everyone or splash them all over social media. This is a private time in your life and only those who are close to you should have access to such personal photos.

Don't feel obligated to answer questions that are inappropriate. It's inevitable that people will ask you insensitive or nosy questions – 'are you carrying twins' or 'wow, how much weight have you gained' can be ignored or brushed off. Strangers will also be more prone to ask you questions you might not want to answer (and you're well within that right!) so you can politely tell them you would rather not share and leave it at that.

Just as there is etiquette for how to have a graceful pregnancy, there are an equal number of guidelines on how to behave when you're around those who are pregnant! Check out some of these tips to remember next time someone decides to share their news with you:

Offer your congratulations and let them know you are happy to hear of their announcement.

Don't ask personal questions – it's insensitive and very private! Questions about whether the couple was trying, the size of the mother's belly, or even about the age of the mother are common questions that don't exhibit proper manners.

Leave the advice to yourself. Every person has tips or advice on how to go through pregnancy or childbirth and beyond, but a pregnant woman is already feeling a multitude of emotions and adding to the stress is not helpful. If the expectant mother comes to you with a question, feel free to share your tips or recommendations, but leave it at that.

Don't feel the need to share your scary experiences or stories you've heard. Pregnancy is an emotional time – especially for those who've dealt with difficulty getting pregnant or complications – so there's no reason for you to create even more anxiety for the mother or couple.

One major faux pas in relation to pregnancy is assuming a woman is pregnant and asking her when she's due! Under no circumstances should you ever ask a woman if she's pregnant because there's often the chance she is not and once you've asked...there's no turning back.

To touch the belly or not touch the belly – some women like it when friends and family touch the belly because it feels like a connection with those they love. Some other women don't like anyone touching their belly! If you find yourself near a pregnant woman and have the impulse to touch their belly always ask for permission before doing so.

As a pregnant woman, you have the right to tell people when you do or don't want them touching your belly – especially strangers who come up to you in the grocery store or at the doctor's office. So how do you politely navigate this area of personal boundaries with grace and elegance? You can:

**Answer them honestly if they ask for permission.** Just because they were polite enough to ask doesn't mean you need to feel obligated to allow them to rub your belly – you can simply say "thank you for asking me, but I would prefer you didn't" or just let them know you don't feel comfortable with anyone touching your belly.

**Step away from their reach.** If confronting someone verbally is too awkward for you, you can make it a point to take a step or two away from them and cover your belly with your hands, then change the focus away from them trying to rub your stomach.

## Etiquette and Adoption

Not every couple is able to have biological children, while some prefer to have children as single parents or even adopt later in life! Those who are going through adoption have a good number of emotional reasons for doing so and the joy of bringing a child into a family is just as special as going through a pregnancy.

It should go without saying that adopted children should be regarded by the extended family on equal status as any biological children. If you're not sure how to properly address the topic of adoption with your loved one or friend, consider these following guidelines:

Adoption is amazing, but don't put unnecessary pressure on the parents as a result of referring to their adoption as a philanthropic situation. It might be natural for you to think that being an adoptive parent is akin to being selfless and an 'angel' for children, but keep in mind that adopting a child for many couples is for the exact same reasons as deciding to try for a biological child – nothing more or less. Don't create a burden to place on parents when they simply want to expand their family.

Let the adoptive parents share their news or journey when they want. The road to adoption is long and emotional – give parents the space and grace to share their journey if and when they want. You wouldn't ask a pregnant woman about the conception or her birth story, so don't ask personal details of an adoptive family, such as were they there for the birth or other questions related to the process.

## Living with Others

At any point in your life, there will likely be others living in your college dorm room, apartment or home. Whether you willingly moved in together or you needed to share the space in order to make it more cost effective, learning how to live with others and stay respectful and graceful does take a bit of work – even if you love the person cohabitating with you, such as a spouse or child!

If you're in the market for roommates, it's important that you take your own lifestyle into consideration before you select someone to live with you. What happens when you like to be in bed by 9 p.m. but your roommate is a night owl and wants friends over every weekend? Or what if you're very tidy by nature, but your roommate likes to be messier?

Understanding your own personality and what you're willing to deal with will help you make a positive choice for a roommate and will allow you to have a more positive experience. Of course, you're not always going to have a say in who lives in your space – such as whether or not you're assigned a roommate in a college dorm or you have to live with others in a military setting. In this case, establishing proper manners and boundaries is a good way to create a comfortable living environment.

No matter what your living situation is, there are three things you need to remember:

- Commitment
- Communication
- Compromise

Once you've signed a contract or a lease, you need to be *committed* to following the house rules if you live with someone or establishing a good living environment for your partner. Check-in with each other periodically to make sure that each of you is doing your fair share and working as a team (or group) to keep the living space clean and welcoming.

*Communication* is key in any relationship, whether it's related to roommates or partners living together. Every person living under the same roof has a responsibility to do what they can to make the home a comfortable and safe place – which is why communication is very helpful. What happens when you do your part, cleaning up after you cook or taking out the trash every evening, but your roommate or partner leaves dirty clothes all over the apartment or forgets to pay the rent despite it being his or her responsibility?

Frequent meetings or chats are helpful in making sure that issues don't go unresolved for a long period of time.

Doing so breeds resentment and eventually anger – so create regular check-ins with each other to ensure that all issues are taken care of in a timely manner.

*Compromise* is another helpful tool in any personal relationship. It helps the overall mood of the house and it can be a realistic option for dealing with some of the most unpleasant tasks – such as you taking out the trash, while the roommate empties the dishwasher each evening. While you might not love doing every single one of your tasks, compromise is more about what you can do to help.

Living together takes an element of respect and trust on both of your parts. Common manners go a long way to creating an environment that benefits everyone living under the same roof.

# Chapter 7

# Entertaining and Hosting Events Elegantly

When one thinks of etiquette, the first thing that typically comes to mind is hosting parties or events inside and outside of the home. As you can see throughout this book, etiquette and manners play a role in nearly every aspect of our lives – from how to properly communicate with your co-worker over the Internet to what to say (or not to say!) to a pregnant woman.

Socializing has been a part of life from the earliest civilizations! The moment someone enters your home, there is a dynamic in play: the role of host and guest. Even if someone wants to come over to watch the big game or to have a simple conversation over a cup of coffee, there are always expectations of both the host and the guest.

## What does it mean to be a host?

When you invite people into your home, you want to give off a sense of welcoming and warmth to your guests. It might be an overwhelming thought to host a number of people over to your home for a celebration, especially when it includes aspects such as:

- Serving food or beverages
- Making sure all your guests are welcomed and introduced to each other
- Setting up the area for the event, whether it's the dining table or an outdoor space

Thinking about all the aspects of a party could feel like a lot to you, but a good thing to remember is that being a gracious host takes all the same manners and etiquette that you exhibit in other areas of your life. What does take a little more care as a host is the planning process and learning how to multitask during the event itself.

As with all things, practice makes perfect. Your very first dinner party might not go as smoothly as you would have hoped, but when things don't go as planned, you're able to take them into consideration for the next event. Did you find yourself too rushed and stressed the day of the event, setting up the party or dinner space? Next time, start the day before and get the table set earlier in the day so you can focus on other aspects of the event.

Planning also means creating a welcoming environment in your space – the group of people you invite has a major impact on the type of party you will have! Fun and interesting guests will turn any event into something amusing and lighthearted, while grumpy and judgmental people will create an element of stress and anxiety for all invited.

So, what makes a good host? Here are some of the most important aspects of proper party planning, which offers plenty of courtesy to guests and helps keep things a little less stressful for you:

**Provide details when sending out the invitation.** Your guests might not like to show up to your event and be completely in the dark – let them know what type of event you're hosting so they can come prepared. If you're hosting a swanky dinner, a printed invitation – which is more formal in style – will highlight the event is a little more important than a football party on the weekend.

**Try to have everything ready before guests arrive.** While there are always last-minute details to fix, make sure you have all the major features completed well before the guests arrive. A good rule of thumb is to be done and dressed for the event no less than 15 minutes before the party begins.

**Create spaces for your guests.** When you're preparing the house for your guests, make sure to go over the spaces they will use and check that everything is in proper order – such as fully-stocked amenities in the guest bathroom, or a clean utility closet for guests to hang coats and handbags.

**Set the tone.** If you welcome your guests to your home like a chicken with your head chopped off, it sets the tone for the entire space and your guests will begin to feel as if they are in your way or a nuisance. Getting ready for the event early also allows you to take a deep breath, have a glass of wine and welcome your guests into a calm and relaxing atmosphere.

Hosting with proper etiquette also means you're the one who will direct the event from start to finish. What does this mean? You'll announce when cocktails are over and dinner begins, as well as when dinner is over. Allow your guests to begin eating after four or five people have been served, so the food does not get cold. A graceful way to begin any dinner party or social event is to start with a toast.

The thought of giving a toast might send shivers down your spine, but it doesn't need to be anything too verbose or complicated. Simply thank your guests for taking the time to come to your home and wish them health and happiness before they dine on your meal. If you're celebrating a special event, a few words regarding why you've gathered everyone together is also a great addition to a toast.

## Keep the Conversation Going

One of the most difficult aspects of hosting is keeping your guests mingling and interacting if they don't know each other. As a host, it's proper etiquette to ensure everyone feels welcomed and a part of the festivities! Just as you will pay close attention to whether your guests are getting enough food or beverages, you'll also want to watch and see that some of your guests are feeling left out of conversations.

Small talk, which we went over in an earlier chapter, is one of the foundations of cocktail parties. Mingling and introducing one another is typical – so there is less for you to do as a host when it comes to keeping the conversation light and friendly. Once the dinner starts, your task will be to keep the lulls in conversation at a minimum – no one likes to eat dinner in silence while at a party! Inevitably, topics of conversation might come up that create a debate amongst guests and while some groups can handle a livelier conversation, it's up to you as a host to keep any topics from getting out of hand, especially if there is a mixed crowd at the table, consisting of old friends and guests who are new to each other.

## Saying Goodbye

Do you find it awkward to tell guests to pack up and leave? At the end of the event, it will be time for guests to leave and you don't want to drag it out. Here are some simple tips you can do in order to wind the party down and let guests know the party is ending:

- Stop serving food or beverages, such as after-dinner coffee or cocktails
- Turn the music off and begin cleaning up the trash around the room
- Tell your guests in a friendly tone that you're exhausted and you have an early start in the morning

## Guest Etiquette

Just as there are tips and guidelines for how to be a proper host, there is an equal number of suggestions and actions for guests. Manners are important no matter where you are – but when you're invited to someone's space, it's vital that you show courtesy and respect. Here are some of the best ways you can show etiquette after you've been invited to a party:

**Be there on time.** Plan your arrival to the event between five and 15 minutes after the start time, but never show up earlier than the time provided on the invitation. This cuts into the time for the host and isn't something he or she should need to accommodate. If you think you'll be more than 15 minutes late, it's respectful to let the host know so they can move on with the festivities or wait for you.

**Don't be on your phone.** It's simply poor etiquette to have your phone go off while you're in a dinner with others. Turn your ringer off and don't answer any calls while you're at the table – if you see that you need to make a call, be sure to excuse yourself from the table and make the call in a different room.

**Be gracious and considerate.** Your host has taken a lot of time and effort to create a dinner party or special event – not to mention the costs included for food and beverages. Always be gracious to the host and thank them for the invitation – it's also kind for you to compliment them on the food choices or the atmosphere!

**Be an active guest.** Whether that means conversing with some new people or playing a silly game with the rest of the guests, do your best to stay a part of the action. Not only does it make the other guests feel inclusive, but it helps alleviate some extra stress for your host if he or she thinks you're not having a good time.

Once you've seen some visible clues that the party is winding down, take it as the opportunity not to wear out your welcome. Proper etiquette highlights that guests can easily stay an hour after the meal to enjoy a coffee or cocktails, then guests should start leaving unless they are invited to stay longer. On your way out the door, be sure to thank the host once again for a pleasant dinner or party – if they're not at the door, then go and look for them to say a personal goodbye.

Does the idea of providing a gift to the host seem confusing? Depending on the reason for the party, a gift might be proper etiquette – such as if it's a housewarming or a special occasion. If you're invited to a dinner party and you don't see each other often, a hostess gift is always welcome and appreciated. The hostess gift doesn't need to be anything too involved – a bouquet of flowers, something small for the house (like a candle) or a nice bottle of wine are all lovely tokens of thanks and are sure to be well received by the host.

# Chapter 8

# Elegance for All Occasions

When you think about all the different events and situations in life, you'll start to realize that manners and etiquette play a major role in nearly everything you do. From traveling to an international country to giving your condolences when someone passes, etiquette is there to provide a foundation for you in order to navigate expectations and to create a universal guide on how to behave with others in mind.

Throughout this book, we've touched upon a number of common events and interactions – from how to behave in a job interview to announcing a wedding! In our final chapter, we'll tie up some loose ends and provide additional guidance on how to manage through some equally important moments.

## Managing Illness and Death

A delicate and difficult time for all involved, illness and death are to be expected at some point in everyone's life.

Offering condolences or dealing with grief is not only extremely hard for most people going through it, but it can also be confusing for those who want to offer sympathy to friends and family but just aren't aware of the proper ways to go about sharing empathy or condolences.

When a loved one is diagnosed with a terminal illness, finding the proper words to express how they feel is sometimes impossible. The important thing to remember is that no matter what you try to say, the best way to let someone know you care is by conveying that you're there for them. During a time of illness, it's not usually about what you can say – it's more about what you can do. Even the smallest acts of kindness, whether it's bringing a cooked meal to a family caring for a sick loved one or spending some time watching a favorite television show with an elder or friend, is a compassionate way to show those in your life that you care.

Sometimes we say things that don't come out correctly. Even when you have the best intention behind what you say, it can often come out wrong or be insensitive. It's also human nature to want to 'solve' problems – whether that's giving someone advice or trying to get them to cheer up when they're feeling depressed, but in the case of managing illness and death, the best course of action is to keep the opinions or advice to yourself. Not that it's coming from a malicious place, but it's important to remember that everyone's dealing with sadness in their own, personal way and what might have worked or helped you might not have the same effect on a friend or loved one.

Death is one of the hardest things to deal with in life and sharing the news is very difficult, but must be done. As with other major life events, notifying the immediate family is number one on the list, followed by close friends. If possible, the notification should be done by someone who is able to contain their composure in order to share the news, as well as any memorial or funeral details that might be set in motion. Once family and friends are notified, announcements can be made in the newspaper or with online memorials, which are often set up through a funeral home.

As with other major announcements, whether or not you want to post the news on social media is up to you. If your loved one or friend was well connected, their social circle would be grateful to learn of the news – but it must certainly be done after all immediate family is notified. No family member wants to find out that news on social media!

If you're the guest to a funeral or memorial service, or you're just at a loss for words and what you can say to help someone understand your empathy, consider some of these options:

**I'm sorry for your loss.** This is a compassionate and simple message that conveys all that you can when trying to comfort someone. Never tell someone that it was 'God's will' or 'what was meant to be' or even the 'she's in a better place' – none of these words are comforting and, in fact, are rather insensitive and can cause unnecessary hurt to someone who's already suffering.

**I'm here for you.** Even if you've been through loss and death on your own, you can never know how someone else feels, so telling them you know how they feel is not ideal. The best way to let your friend or family know that you are there for them is to express that you are available for meals or other specific tasks at any time.

If you're a guest at a funeral or memorial service and it's a religious ceremony outside of your own customs, be willing to ask a funeral director or close friend what you must do to show respect in a house of worship. Whether it's a Jewish funeral, Christian service or a Muslim memorial, be sure to do your research on how to interact with others and follow proper customs that are respectful to that particular religion.

When you're not particularly close to someone who's passed away but you want to show support for a friend or co-worker, a note of condolence or sympathy is a polite and compassionate thing to do when you've heard the news. These notes are best sent within a week of the announcement but can be written at any time if the news hasn't reached you until later.

## Children and Etiquette

One of the best ways to ensure that proper manners and etiquette are passed on is to start teaching children at an early age. Even as young as one year, you can begin teaching children about manners by using them yourself! Children learn by example, so the best way to get them to understand about being considerate and respectful is to use those exact same manners yourself.

So, what can you do when you have a young baby in the house? Start with some of these behaviors as early as possible so they become engrained in a child's upbringing:

**Always use manners.** Even when communicating with your baby, add the words 'please' and 'thank you' to actions and requests that you direct toward time. If you are consistent about using these words from an early age, they will learn them as second nature and will be much more likely to use them on their own.

**Implement table manners.** Placing a bib on a child and teaching them to use a spoon is one of the first steps into learning proper table manners. Encouraging your child to wash their hands and eat with silverware is a great step in taking care during a meal. Also, as an adult, it's your responsibility to set the tone for a proper meal – which means no television or phones at the table.

As children get older, these foundations can be built up even further. For example, after learning how to use a plastic spoon and chew with their mouth closed as a toddler, the next step is to hold silverware properly and even begin using a butter knife if dexterity allows for it at six to 10 years of age.

Once a child hits the teenage years, more boundaries and rules are set into place to teach a variety of life lessons – communicating with parents, sharing and being respectful of boundaries, as well as learning how to spend more time with friends and away from the watchful eye of parents. When a child finally hits early adulthood, it's with the hope that they take all of the discipline and manners they've learned growing up and implement it into daily life as they head off to college, look for jobs and even plan for their own milestones.

## Acting Gracefully Never Stops

If you think that etiquette is learned as a child and then you never need to learn anything about manners again, you're wrong! Even as an individual hits their golden years and beyond, there are still guidelines for proper behavior. Life expectancy has made it so that we are living into our 80s and beyond – and the significant life changes that take place should also be managed with grace and elegance.

Depending on whether a senior lives in a community home or independently, there are a number of ways for navigating the need for help while also being respectful for those who are giving care (as well as caregivers giving proper respect to elders):

**Don't just expect the help.** If you're a senior who needs help getting groceries or cleaning the house, it's a good idea to ask for assistance rather than expect it to happen. As important as your tasks are, caregivers do lead their own lives and have plenty of things to take care of on a personal level, so you can't expect them to know when you need assistance at all times. Asking for help instead of expecting it also shows respect and consideration for those who are willing to put aside their needs to help.

**Give thanks.** Even if you're engaging with a caregiver on a daily basis and it's 'their job' to assist you, thankfulness is a trait that goes a long way in making someone feel happy about helping. Don't assume they know you're thankful – it's always nice to get that positive reinforcement.

**Stay active.** Whether you're living in an assisted community or at home, one of the best ways to stay mentally and physically healthy is by participating in activities – groups such as a book club, senior exercise class, or even a craft club allow you to socialize and stay cognitively healthy into your golden years.

There also comes a time when you or a caregiver will need to have a difficult conversation with a loved one. Caring for someone takes a toll on a caregiver mentally, emotionally and physically and sometimes it's better for all involved to have something more official set in place to help manage with care.

Talking about assisted living, legal changes and even end-of-life changes is hard to talk about but must be done for the sake of your senior family member, as well as your peace of mind. Speak with your elder's doctor to learn about the best course of action in terms of treatment or long-term care. If you're a caregiver, your health and mental capacity also need to be cared for with compassion. Be sure to:

> *Get the proper amount of sleep and rest that you can*
>
> *Don't be afraid to ask for help – you can't do everything on your own*
>
> *Take periods of respite so you can get a break from the stress*

If you know someone in the family is acting as a caregiver, the thoughtful thing to do is to reach out when you can and let them know you're there to offer support and help when you can. Be available for making plans and help provide relief at times for the caregiver so they can maintain their own health.

# Conclusion

As you have seen by now, elegance can be a major part of daily life. When you're at the grocery store and you nearly run into someone with a cart, do you say 'excuse me' as if it's second nature? Do you hold the door open for someone coming in from behind you?

When you host a party, do you go out of your way to ensure your guests don't sit in silence at the table or do you tell your child to mind his or her manners and chew with their mouth closed?

All of these scenarios are a matter of acting gracefully and while you might know some, hopefully, there have been some instances throughout this book where you learned what to say (and what not to say!) to someone going through pregnancy or a death in the family.

Etiquette isn't just something you learn once and then have that knowledge forever – it's constantly changing to accommodate the modern world and all of the updates within it, such as technology! This is evident as you explore the type of etiquette that took place in the Victorian Age and what's considered etiquette in the 21st century. Whether you're a child, an adult or a senior, there are plenty of guidelines and manners for interacting with others and providing respect and consideration. Ultimately, no matter where you travel or how young and old you are, manners and etiquette are universal amongst humans.

Now that you've gotten an idea as to just how much etiquette plays a role in our daily life and with everyone that we come across, it is our hope that you continue learning and understanding the various tips and recommendations for different areas of your life. Whether it's throwing a wedding or baby shower or learning how to tip at restaurants and taking public transportation, the ways in which you can grow and be a more graceful and elegant person is endless – which all of us benefit from learning such foundations in etiquette.

One last thing!

I want to give you a **one-in-two-hundred chance** to win a **$200.00 Amazon Gift card** as a thank-you for reading this book.

All I ask is that you give me some feedback, so I can improve this or my next book :)

Your opinion is *super valuable* to me. It will only take a minute of your time to let me know what you like and what you didn't like about this book. The hardest part is deciding how to spend the two hundred dollars! Just follow this link.

# http://reviewers.win/actelegantly